Birds Make Nests

Birds Make Nests

Mute Swan

MICHAEL GARLAND

Holiday House / New York

The publisher thanks Dr. Alexandra M. Class Freeman and Dr. Paul R. Sweet for reviewing this book.

This book supports the Next Generation Science Standards for Life Science for grade 1 (Structure and Function, Growth and Development of Organisms and Information Processing) and for Engineering Design for grades K-2. It can also support Science, Technology, Engineering and Mathematics curriculums.

Black-capped
Chickadee

Library of Congress Cataloging-in-Publication Data
Names: Garland, Michael, 1952- author, illustrator.
Title: Birds make nests / Michael Garland.
Description: First edition. | New York : Holiday House, [2017]
Identifiers: LCCN 2016004461 | ISBN 9780823436620 (hardcover)
Subjects: LCSH: Birds—Nests—Juvenile literature. |
Bird—Behavior—Juvenile literature.
Classification: LCC QL675 .G37 2017 | DDC 598.156/4—dc23 LC record available at
https://lccn.loc.gov/2016004461

For Donna

Mourning Dove

Birds make nests.

Painted Bunting (Male)

(Female)

Some nests are high.

Osprey

Some nests are low.

Australian
Pelican

Northern
Cardinal
(Male)

(Female)

These nests are shaped like cups.

Ruby-throated
Hummingbird
(Male)

(Female)

These nests are shaped like mounds.

American
Flamingo

Some birds make nests on the ground.

Common
Ostrich

Great
Horned
Owl

Some birds make nests in holes in trees.

Atlantic Puffin

Some birds make nests in burrows on grassy slopes.

Some birds make nests that hang.
This bird makes its nest with grass and animal hair.
The hole is at the top.

Baltimore Oriole
(Male)

This bird makes its nest with sticks and leaves.
The hole is at the bottom.

verdin

This bird uses mud to close a hole in a tree.
The female stays in the tree.
The male has to feed her.

Great Hornbill

And this bird uses a snakeskin to keep predators away.

Great Crested
Flycatcher

These birds make one big nest.

Sociable
Weaver

But some birds don't make nests.
This bird lays its eggs in other birds' nests.

Brown-
headed
Cowbird

Thrush
Nightingale

House
Finch

Barn Owl

House
Sparrow

Birds make many kinds of nests in many kinds of places.

Canada
Goose

Western
Bluebird

White Stork

Bald Eagle

Birds make nests to keep eggs safe . . .

and to keep chicks safe.

American Robin

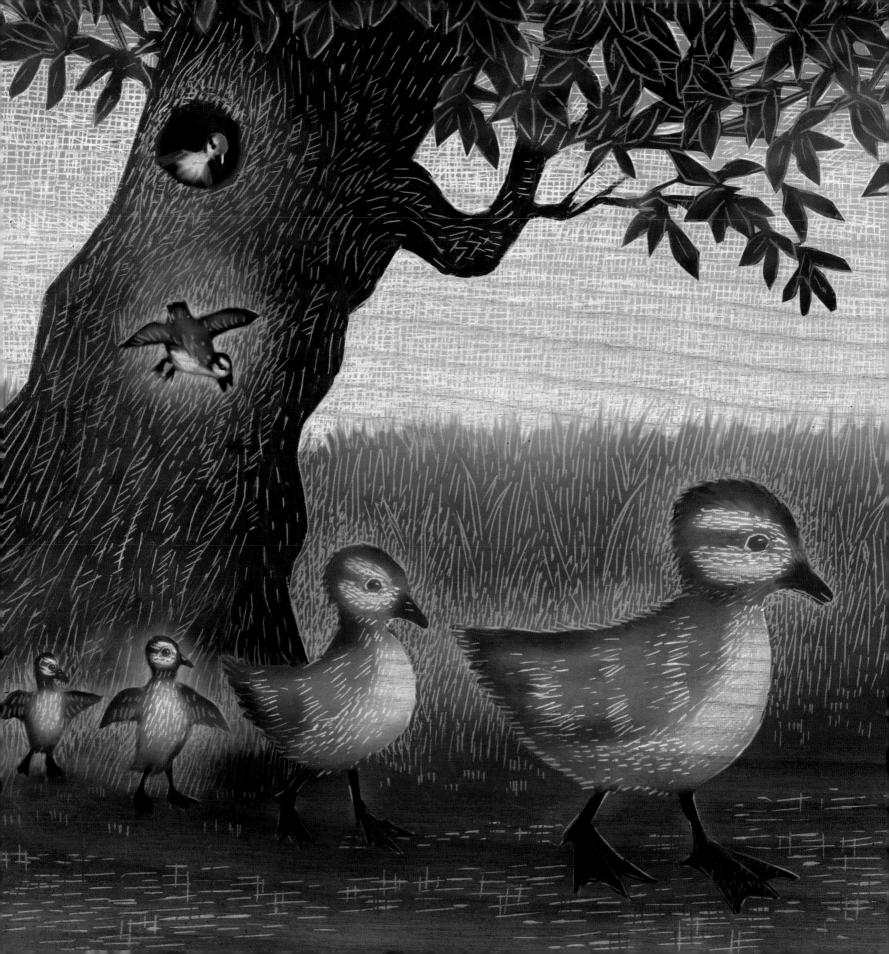

And one day chicks leave their nest.

Wood Duck
(Female)

Common Loon